TULSA CITY-COUNTY LIBRARY

hrjc

D1243508

SEP – – 2020

TULSA CITY-COUNTY LIBRARY

WORLD *of* GLASS

THE ART OF DALE CHIHULY

by **JAN GREENBERG** and **SANDRA JORDAN**

ABRAMS BOOKS FOR YOUNG READERS • NEW YORK

Cataloging-in-Publication Data has been
applied for and may be obtained from the
Library of Congress.

ISBN 978-1-4197-3681-0

Text copyright © 2020 Jan Greenberg
and Sandra Jordan
All artwork and images copyright
© Chihuly Studio
Page 7, photo of Japanese floats:
age fotostock / Alamy Stock Photo
Edited by Howard W. Reeves
Book design by Katie Benezra

Published in 2020 by Abrams Books for
Young Readers, an imprint of ABRAMS. All
rights reserved. No portion of this book may
be reproduced, stored in a retrieval system,
or transmitted in any form or by any means,
mechanical, electronic, photocopying,
recording, or otherwise, without written
permission from the publisher.

Printed and bound in China
10 9 8 7 6 5 4 3 2 1

Abrams Books for Young Readers are
available at special discounts when
purchased in quantity for premiums and
promotions as well as fundraising or
educational use. Special editions can also be
created to specification. For details, contact
specialsales@abramsbooks.com or the
address below.

Abrams® is a registered trademark of
Harry N. Abrams, Inc.

ABRAMS The Art of Books
195 Broadway, New York, NY 10007
abramsbooks.com

ABOVE: Dale Chihuly with *Isola di San Giacomo in Palude Chandelier*, Venice, Italy, 1996

PREVIOUS PAGE: Dale Chihuly at the United World College drawing workshop, Armand Hammer United World College of the American West, Montezuma, New Mexico, 2000

CONTENTS

Dale Chihuly, Nuutajärvi, Finland, 1995

PROLOGUE
FOLLOWING YOUR NOSE

"I think water inspires extraordinary creativity."
—Dale Chihuly

1995. Dale Chihuly stood on a bridge in Finland, holding a bright blue piece of glass bigger than a watermelon. He and his expert American glassblowers had spent days working in tandem with the team at Nuutajärvi, a historic Finnish glass factory.

"Come on sweetheart," he crooned to the glass. "One, two, three." He heaved it into the slow-moving river, where it hit with a splash and settled. The glass didn't break. It floated, and Dale gleefully tossed another piece over the bridge railing.

LEFT: Collecting *Cobalt Belugas* from river rock, Nuutajärvi, Finland, 1995

RIGHT: Leslie Jackson and Dale Chihuly, Nuutajärvi, Finland, 1995

Dale Chihuly, *Carnival Boat*, 2002, 4 x 15 x 5 ft.,
Fairchild Tropical Botanic Garden, Coral Gables,
Florida, installed 2006

Chihuly and hotshop team, Nuutajärvi Glass, Nuutajärvi, Finland, 1995

The glistening objects, named *Belugas* by his team, spun in the current, catching and reflecting the morning sunshine. "Makes this river come to life," Dale said. He threw in more and more glass until the river was full of bobbing blue and red *Belugas*. Dale had thrown so many off the bridge that he drafted a group of teenagers from the nearby town to help collect the *Belugas* and pile them into rowboats. "They looked so stunning," Dale said. "This was a new idea for me." It's one he still uses today.

The summer days were long in Finland. Dale moved back and forth between hanging artworks in the surrounding forest and going to the glass factory, where he could let his imagination run free.

The lead glassblowers, called gaffers, and the crew labored to keep up with Dale's energy. He liked the results of working fast, pushing a piece of glass to the limit. When Dale stood next to a gaffer blowing a hot piece of glass, he would encourage him to stretch the piece longer, to make a bigger bulb on the end. "He was right there, working with us, telling us what he wanted to do," the gaffer recalled. "It was an exciting time."

The world calls him:

Magician

Artist

Marvel

Phenomenon

Entrepreneur

Showman

Living Legend

His teams call him Maestro.

CHAPTER 1
CHILDHOOD DAYS

"Since I was a little boy I always loved glass."
—Dale Chihuly

Dale Chihuly was born in 1941 in Tacoma, Washington. Things were very different in the 1940s and 1950s. There were no computers, no cell phones, and no video games. Televisions were in black and white with few stations and small screens. But some things were the same. Kids rode their bikes around the neighborhood and played games

LEFT: Clockwise from back left: Viola Chihuly, George S. Chihuly, George W. Chihuly, and Dale Chihuly, Tacoma, Washington, c. 1946

RIGHT: Viola Chihuly and Dale Chihuly, Tacoma, Washington, c. 1983

W. W. Seymour Botanical Conservatory, Tacoma, Washington, 2008

at home with their families. When Dale was little, his mother, Viola, said he sat on the floor for hours drawing happily with crayons. She never suspected that he would grow up to be a famous artist.

One of Dale's favorite outings was going with his mother to the W. W. Seymour Botanical Conservatory, a glasshouse in Tacoma. The two liked to roam through the rooms of exotic plants and lush displays of flowers.

Although their house was modest in size, Dale's mother surrounded it with a blossoming garden filled with hydrangeas, rhododendrons, and tulips. At dusk on most evenings, she would ring a bell,

the signal for her young sons, Dale and his older brother, George, to come home. Dale, six years younger, looked up to his popular, athletic brother. George often let Dale tag along with him. Together with their mom, the boys would climb the hill near their house to watch the sunset paint the sky pink, yellow, and orange.

Years later when Dale achieved fame for his vibrant glass artwork, he talked about his mother's love of color and how it influenced him.

"I like to say I've never met a color I didn't like."

On weekends the family would go to the beach on Puget Sound. Dale searched for sea glass, worn

Dale Chihuly, *Niijima Floats*, 2005, Fairchild Tropical Botanic Garden, Coral Gables, Florida

TOP: Dale Chihuly, Tacoma, Washington, c. 1951

ABOVE: Japanese floats

into smooth frosted shapes by the ocean waves. A special find was a glass float in blue, green, or white. Floats that broke away from the fishing nets of Japanese trawlers drifted on the Pacific Ocean currents to the Washington beaches. One day, in a place far away from Tacoma, these floats would inspire Dale's art.

His father, George Senior, an organizer for the meatpackers' union, worked hard but the family was far from rich. Even in elementary school Dale tried to help out by making his own spending money. He and his friends played marbles during their lunch periods. He became so expert that he always won, knocking the others' marbles right out of the ring. Since the winner takes the loser's marbles, Dale walked home every afternoon with his pockets bulging. His mother sewed little bags, which she filled with the multicolored glass balls, and then tied them up with string. At school the next day Dale sold the bags of marbles back to his friends. Then they played all over again.

During summer vacation when Dale was eleven, he had the bright idea to open a lawn-mowing business. "I went from house to house, asking neighbors if they needed their grass cut. Then I sent the other boys around to do the mowing." Dale paid his friends but kept a small commission from each job for himself.

Dale's childhood seemed idyllic, walking to and from his neighborhood school, playing with his big brother, and going on excursions with his parents. All that would soon change.

Dale Chihuly, *The Chihuly Window*, 2000,
19½ x 17 ft., University of Puget Sound,
Tacoma, Washington

CHAPTER 2
GROWING UP OR WHEN LIFE GIVES YOU LEMONS

"I don't think much about the past; I think more about the future."
—Dale Chihuly

Viola Chihuly and Dale Chihuly, 1965

At age twenty-one, Dale's brother George died. After enlisting in the navy to earn a college scholarship, he was killed in a flight-training accident. The next year Dale's father, only fifty-one, died of a heart attack. These tragedies so close together devastated Dale and his mother. Now they were a family of two.

His father's death left them in debt. Dale's mother, who had always been a stay-at-home mom, took a job pouring beer in a tavern nearby.

Dale said, "She didn't make much but she would have given me anything. She never spent money on herself. You couldn't even buy her a dress."

"She was a great mother, in truth, a very lenient mother, an if-you're-going-to-do-something-wrong-you-should-do-it-at-home kind of mother."

For that reason there were always kids hanging out at the Chihuly house. Dale said he wasn't a good student and admitted his pals were a wild crowd. For the most part he managed to stay out of trouble, but "sometimes we put out a street light—my first work in glass."

With his dark, curly hair and big smile, Dale was a charmer, more interested in girls and cars than schoolwork. "I played some sports. I played golf and tennis, but I didn't care for studying and I didn't study in high school." But Ma Chihuly, as she was affectionately called, believed in her son and wanted him to be the best he could be.

"My mother never came down on me very hard and never, ever told me what to do. Later, when she asked me to go to college, it was a big deal."

"I don't know how we're going to make it," Ma Chihuly told him, "but we are—so just get over there and register." She persuaded him to enroll at College of Puget Sound (now University of Puget Sound) in his hometown. At seventeen, younger than most students in age and looks, Dale started his college career. He paid his way by working a variety of jobs: Busing in a restaurant. Selling clothes at Bernie's Men's Store. Switching trains for the railroad. Working on the meat-packing line at a slaughterhouse.

As a freshman, he took his first course in weaving "because I knew there would be a lot of girls in the class." At home he remodeled his mother's basement into what then was called a rec room. "I did sort of '50s modern drapes . . . and I made my own furniture. So I thought I was this cool interior designer."

He transferred to the department of architecture and interior design at the University of Washington

Dale Chihuly, University of Washington, Seattle, c. 1961

in Seattle. "I unfortunately joined a fraternity house and that put me sort of in the party mode. A couple of years later I'm still not studying and I'm twenty-one years old and halfway through college. I know I'm going to be a mediocre something."

Dale realized he was wasting time and money. Longing for adventure, he sold his VW Beetle, and, with Ma Chihuly's blessing, took off for Europe, "just traveling, wandering."

Dale Chihuly with *Glass Wall Installation*, Seattle, 1965

CHAPTER 3
TURNING POINT

"I remember arriving at the kibbutz as a boy of twenty-one and leaving a man, just a few short months later." —Dale Chihuly

1962. A cold winter in Europe.

In those days Europe cost less than the United States, but Dale stretched the seventy-five-dollar monthly allowance his mother sent him to the limit. "Sometimes I would be able to last and sometimes I would run out of money and go hungry for a day or two." After spending several chilly months in Paris, Dale headed south to Italy where he thought he might learn Italian. "I was never very good at languages," he admitted. Eventually he

LEFT: Dale Chihuly traveling in Turkey, 1963

RIGHT: Kibbutz Lahav in Israel, 1963

Weaving with Fused Glass, 1965, in Viola Chihuly's dining room, Tacoma, Washington

found his way to Greece. The weather was so cold that when Dale hitched a ride in a VW, he wrapped himself in a sleeping bag to keep warm. At the Acropolis in Athens it started snowing. Dale took off again, searching for the sun, visited Turkey, and ended up in Israel.

He stayed at Kibbutz Lahav, a communal settlement, in the hot Negev desert. Dale was attracted to the idea of people living and working together communally, farming the land, and sharing profits.

The younger members of Lahav were expected to guard the boundaries of the kibbutz, which was close to the border with Jordan.

"I discovered there was more to life than having a good time," said Dale. "It had a lot to do with going out on border patrol during the night with guys my own age who had more responsibility and maturity than adults twice their age in the United States. After the kibbutz experience, my life would never be the same."

Dale returned home determined "to make some sort of contribution to society." The first step was to finish his college degree. Back at the University of Washington in a course on weaving, he experimented with interlacing small bits of glass with copper wire into the fabric. He won the Seattle Weavers Guild Award.

TOP: Dale Chihuly working as a commercial fisherman in Alaska, 1966

ABOVE: Dale Chihuly, Flora C. Mace, Benjamin Moore, and Therman Statom, Rhode Island School of Design, Providence

After graduation, Dale found a job as a designer with a top Seattle architecture firm. A friend of his dad let him stay in his basement, where Dale set up a studio. His big purchase was a small kiln for melting glass to shape into pieces for his woven tapestries. One night, on a whim, he dipped a piece of plumber's pipe into the melted glass and puffed air into it. Suddenly a bubble appeared.

"To this day, I have never gotten over the excitement of molten glass . . . the process is so wonderfully simple, yet so mystifying . . . I'm still amazed to see the first breath of air enter the hot gather of glass at the end of a blowpipe." At age twenty-three, Dale discovered what would be his lifelong passion.

Obsessed with learning everything he could about blowing glass, he applied for graduate studies at the University of Wisconsin, which offered the only glassblowing program in the country. To earn money for tuition, he quit his design job and signed on to a commercial fishing boat headed for Alaska. Rough, tough, and dangerous! But the pay was excellent.

At the end of the fishing season, he found out he'd been granted a fellowship plus a teaching assistantship. It turned out that all his hard-earned money wasn't needed. Dale moved to the University of Wisconsin in Madison, determined "to blow glass full time."

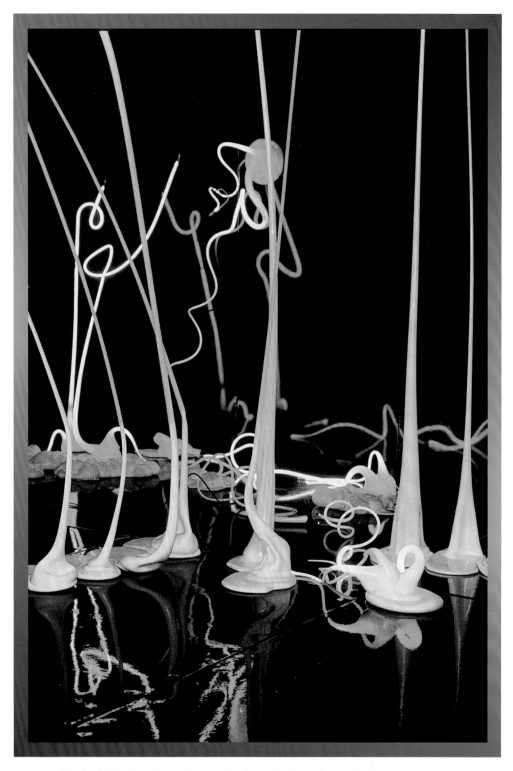

Dale Chihuly, *Glass Forest #1*, in collaboration with James Carpenter at RISD, 1971–72, 500 square ft., Museum of Contemporary Crafts, New York

That year set Dale on a new path, studying glassblowing. From there he went on to earn a second master's degree, one from Rhode Island School of Design (RISD). He plunged into an exploration of non-traditional ways of glassblowing.

When Dale applied to work with glassblowers in Venice, Italy, the world-renowned Venini factory accepted him, and he received a Fulbright fellowship to finance his study. But it didn't go smoothly.

"When I got there, I didn't know the city. I was supposed to know Italian but I didn't. I was in a funk. So I wandered around Venice from September until December." Dale felt depressed and these episodes would bother him more and more as he grew older.

Around Christmastime he finally worked up the energy to turn up at the factory. He met the owner who said Venini had been offered a commission, a competition for a piece of sculpture. "I was too intimidated to blow glass myself because I was such a lousy glass blower compared to the great ones there." However, he wasn't too intimidated to design a sculpture.

Venini won and Dale was given a little studio. Now he had the chance to be with glassblowers and designers. "I watched and I learned and I saw the teams in action. By the time I went home I started using the information." Back in the United States, he accepted a teaching position at RISD, where he made use of teamwork for his own experiments with glassblowing.

Organic or natural shapes intrigued Dale the most. He pushed to see how far molten glass could stretch by pulling the hot strands. Sometimes he stood on a ladder to watch the shapes elongate and fall to the floor. He and fellow sculptor and collaborator James Carpenter incorporated neon gas to light the glass from within. *Glass Forest #1* became their first sculptural installation (see page 15).

During his years at RISD, he established a glassblowing program and created forms in glass both unique and ambitious. These pieces led to many innovative artworks in the future. Made in collaboration with James Carpenter at RISD, *20,000 Pounds of Ice and Neon* inspired a huge ice sculpture in Jerusalem almost twenty years later.

Although Dale spent most of his time in Providence, his heart belonged to the Pacific Northwest where he grew up. He often returned home to visit his mother and see old friends.

Dale Chihuly, *20,000 Pounds of Ice and Neon* (detail), in collaboration with James Carpenter, 1971, 600 square ft., Rhode Island School of Design, Woods-Gerry Gallery, Providence

Pilchuck Glass School with student artwork,
Stanwood, Washington, 1993

CHAPTER 4
CHALLENGES

"I learned from other artists that it wasn't that hard to make art. You do what you want to do. You just have to have the confidence to do it." —Dale Chihuly

1971. Fifty miles from Seattle, on a tree farm owned by local art patrons, Dale and a group of artists and students built a school for the glass arts. It was located in the foothills of the Cascade Range. They named the school Pilchuck, which translates as "red water" from the language of the Chinook, the Native Americans who live in the area. At first, the conditions were primitive. People slept under plastic tarps draped over planks.

Pilchuck Glass School, Stanwood, Washington, 1971

Dale Chihuly, *Artpark Installation #4*, in collaboration with Seaver Leslie, 1975, Lewiston, New York

The makeshift hotshop where Chihuly and several others taught glassblowing was a big open-air tent. The sixteen students' first project was to build a furnace to melt glass and ovens to reheat it.

There was no running water or plumbing at Pilchuck, but the site was beautiful, with rolling hills, tall pine trees, and a pond. It evolved into the best art school for glass in the world.

Early in the summer of 1975 Dale received a grant to go to Artpark, a music-and-art destination in upstate New York. On 172 acres, Dale and fellow artist Seaver Leslie installed a temporary outdoor piece consisting of large, intensely colored panes of glass. For days the two men moved the glass to different locations—ponds, hillsides, trees—observing and photographing the changing light both through the glass and reflected in the water.

With his reputation growing, Dale traveled the world, sharing his skills and learning from other glassblowers. Life was going well until a dark, rainy night in England. The car he was riding in crashed and Dale was thrown through the windshield.

Along with 253 stitches in his face and many painful days in the hospital, he lost sight in one eye. Dale said, "There was no despair because I just felt so lucky that I didn't lose both my eyes." Instead of an artificial eye, he put on a swashbuckling black eye patch. It became one of his trademarks.

"It probably made me realize how vulnerable one is. It might have made me more of a risk taker. I don't think you become a very good artist if you can't."

Dale Chihuly in dark glasses over his eye patch in the RISD hotshop, c. 1983

Dale went on blowing glass for a while. But molten glass is hot at 2,100 degrees Fahrenheit. Swinging a blowpipe is a physical action that requires his team to move in a coordinated way. With sight in only one eye, Dale lacked depth perception. Judging distances accurately was hard. The group in the hotshop worried that he couldn't always see them.

After dislocating his shoulder in an accident while body surfing, Dale finally gave up blowing glass. He assumed the role of director, making drawings in the hotshop to pass along ideas to his team. His ability to lead, as well as to spot talent, revitalized him.

A glassblower who often worked with Dale said, "The thing I found most remarkable about the whole situation was just his incredible strength, his astonishing ability to bounce back in full force like nothing had happened."

CHAPTER 5
BLOWBLOWBLOW

"I don't care what people call them—containers, sculpture, craft, fine art—as long as they're given as much consideration as other objects that represent the maker's feelings and ideas."
—Dale Chihuly

Dale Chihuly painting on the Boathouse deck, Seattle, 1993

TOP: **Northwest Room with some of Dale Chihuly's collections, including a birch bark canoe, the Boathouse, Seattle, 1999**

ABOVE: **The Boathouse hotshop with Dale Chihuly's drawings on the wall, Seattle, 1991**

1998 to the present.

Off a busy street in Seattle, down a gravel driveway, unnoticeable unless you're looking for it, is Dale Chihuly's Boathouse. Once a factory that built racing shells, the building overlooks Lake Union with its mix of motorboats, tugboats, and barges. Rising above the lake is the Ship Canal Bridge. Dale built a hotshop, studio, and private galleries to exhibit his work and collections of Americana.

The hotshop is the main place where he directs his teams, which can include anywhere from six to fifteen people. There Dale makes fast drawings and hangs them up to guide his team. At various times he's used pastel sticks, black charcoal, or liquid latex. "Most of the drawings are quite spontaneous. I don't do much with preconceived ideas."

Paula Stokes, who runs the hotshop, said, "He is interested in our opinions. He brings people together, the best people he can find to enrich his ideas. We work within an established vocabulary, Dale's vocabulary."

TOP: The first gather of molten glass in a pipe.
The Boathouse hotshop, Seattle, 2017

ABOVE: Reheating in the furnace. The Boathouse hotshop,
Seattle, 2013

ABOVE: Shaping glass using an optic mold.
The Boathouse hotshop, Seattle, 1995

William Morris spins the molten glass as Dale Chihuly shapes it with wooden paddles. Pilchuck Glass School, Stanwood, Washington, 1983

A grapefruit-size ball of red-hot glass is gathered from the furnace on the end of a stainless steel pipe. A single breath is blown into the pipe to form a small bubble. Depending on the effect the glassblower wants to achieve, crushed glass color is placed on a steel table where the hot glass is rolled into it. More air is added, and then the gather goes back into the oven for one last layer of molten glass. The glass is constantly reheated in a furnace to keep it hot and liquid. The hot glass is shaped as the pipe is rotated round and round. What happens? The sides spin out, pulled by centrifugal force, like a dancer's skirt when she twirls around.

Dale prefers to use as few tools as possible, to let the heat, gravity, and glassblowers do their magic. But there are some basics: a blowpipe, a blowtorch, wooden paddles, jacks (large tweezers), and glassblowing molds.

When the piece is finished, one of the team carries it quickly and carefully over to the cooling oven. The glass is so hot that protective gear resembling an astronaut's suit is needed. A piece can take twelve hours or more to cool down.

Dale Chihuly, Joslyn Art Museum, Omaha, Nebraska, 2000

James Mongrain, shaping glass using gravity and centrifugal force. The Boathouse hotshop, Seattle, 2013

James Mongrain, Eric Pauli, and Dale Chihuly, the Boathouse hotshop, Seattle, 2000

Two members of the team dressed in protective suits carry the hot glass to the annealing oven where it will cool for up to twenty-four hours. Dale Chihuly and the hotshop team, the Boathouse hotshop, Seattle, 1992

TOP: Flora C. Mace, Dale Chihuly, and Joey Kirkpatrick, Pilchuck Glass School, Stanwood, Washington, 1987

ABOVE: Joey Kirkpatrick, Heather Gray, Flora C. Mace, William Morris, Raven Skyriver, Alex Stisser, and Kelly O'Dell, Museum of Glass, Tacoma, Washington, 2006

CHAPTER 6

WHAT IS A SERIES? HOW DOES IT WORK?

"Imagine the sand turns into liquid. Stick a pipe in there, gather it up like honey, and bring it out. Blow in there and you can make an incredible array of new forms just using human breath."
—Dale Chihuly

Think of the World Series in baseball or the Harry Potter books and films. A series in art has to do with the creation of many different artworks unified around the same theme. In Dale's series, each piece is different, yet related by theme and process. Traditional glass factory production was about creating perfectly formed identical vessels. Dale's work represents a departure from the past.

Here is a selection of his series.

TOP: Dale Chihuly, *Black Cylinders*, 2006. These cylinders are symmetrical, which means if you draw a line down the middle, both sides are the same—they match.

ABOVE: Dale Chihuly, *Rose Dore Soft Cylinder with Chartreuse Drawing*, 1986, 17 x 14 x 13 in. This cylinder is asymmetrical, meaning the two sides are different.

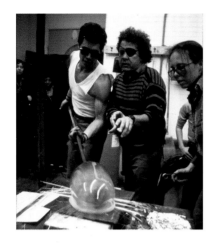

TOP: **William Morris, Dale Chihuly, and Flora C. Mace, Carnegie Mellon University, Pittsburgh, 1985**

ABOVE LEFT: **Northwest Native American baskets**

RIGHT: **Dale Chihuly,** *Tangerine Basket Set with Raven Lip Wraps,* **2002, 19 x 22 x 18 in.**

CYLINDERS 1975

On a trip to Santa Fe, Dale began collecting Navajo blankets and early trade blankets, which were used to barter for supplies with Native Americans. The vivid colors and woven patterns inspired his *Cylinder* series.

With a team of glassblowers at Pilchuck, Dale developed a "pick-up" technique for the intricate designs of the *Cylinders*. This involved laying glass threads on a steel table, called a marver, and picking them up with molten glass. The next year, the Metropolitan Museum in New York City acquired three *Navajo Blanket Cylinders* for their collection—a first for Dale.

BASKETS 1977

When Chihuly saw Northwest Native American baskets at the Washington State History Museum, he was intrigued. He would capture in glass the way these handwoven baskets slump under their own weight.

SEAFORMS 1980

Ever since he was a boy living near Puget Sound, Dale has had a passion for water. "I pushed the idea of the transparency of glass and sea and water and ice and it all fit together in the *Seaforms*." The pieces look like "something that came from the sea." He wanted viewers to wonder, is it manmade or natural?

LEFT: Dale Chihuly, *Pearl and Oxblood Seaform Set*, 1982

LEFT INSET: Dale Chihuly, *Seaform/Basket Drawing*, 1981, 30 x 22 in.

RIGHT: Color rods used to color the molten glass, the Boathouse hotshop, Seattle

MACCHIA ("SPOT" IN ITALIAN) 1981

Dale began this series with the idea of using all three hundred hues of the color rods on his shelves in the hotshop. "Some of the color combinations I thought would be ugly turned out to be the very best . . . You can't exhaust the color possibilities."

Dale Chihuly, *Macchia*, 1983, Pilchuck Glass School, Stanwood, Washington

Dale Chihuly, *Persian Ceiling*, 1999, 15 x 28 in., de Young Museum, San Francisco, California, installed 2008

LEFT: Dale Chihuly, *Lap Pool*, 1994, 12 x 54 x 4 ft., the Boathouse, Seattle

RIGHT: Dale Chihuly, *Putti in Nest Kissing Opalescent Hummingbird on Orange Vessel*, 1999, 28 x 16 x 16 in.

PERSIANS 1986

In the mid-eighties, Dale spent a year with one of his teams blowing more than one thousand experimental miniature pieces. By the end of that year, they had created a new series he named *Persians* to honor his love of Venice and the Far East. That year of testing produced one of his most popular series.

PUTTI 1989

Putti, Italian for "cherubs," were modeled out of molten glass. "Normally I don't like the looks of figures in glass," said Dale. But he felt these tubby little rascals added fun to his work. He joked that they looked a lot like him. The *Putti* are often attached to vessels, hanging topsy-turvy, mingling with glass flowers, birds, or sea creatures.

ABOVE: Dale Chihuly, *Mottled Bronze Ikebana with Apricot and Chartreuse Stems*, 1998, 68 x 28 x 14 in, Missouri Botanical Garden, St. Louis, installed 2006

RIGHT: Dale Chihuly, *Torchier*, 1997, 11 x 6 x 6 ft, Franklin Park Conservatory, Columbus, Ohio, installed 2003

Dale Chihuly, *Niijima Floats*, 1992, Honolulu Academy of Arts

IKEBANA 1989

Ikebana is the art of flower arranging in Japan. Dale said, "If the piece has separate parts coming out of it, it's called *Ikebana*." Sometimes he added sunflower shapes to the vessels, a nod to Vincent van Gogh, one of his favorite artists. In later *Ikebana*, the forms became more free-flowing—rising out of bulbous vases or long spheres that were brought together into his larger groupings of glass sculpture.

FIORI ("FLOWERS" IN ITALIAN) 2003

Some of Dale's happiest memories as a child centered on times he spent with his mother in her year-round garden. When people come across his *Fiori* in a flower bed or glasshouse, they can't help but smile. These forms were given light-hearted names, such as *Frog Feet*, *Reeds*, *Fiddleheads*, *Seal Pups*, *Walla Wallas*, and *Herons*.

NIIJIMA FLOATS 1991

This series looks like giant marbles or big glass beach balls. The form reminded Dale of the Japanese fishing floats he collected as a child. Don't let the simple form fool you. It's difficult to blow a piece of glass so big and round. "We don't know if it will break," said Chihuly. "I make the team go beyond what they can do. It makes it more interesting."

CHAPTER 7

GLASSHOUSES, GARDENS, ANCIENT SITES AND NEW ONES

"What makes the Chandeliers *work for me is the massing of color. When you take hundreds of pieces of blown glass of one color, put them together, and then shoot light through them, something extraordinary happens."* —Dale Chihuly

Dale woke up one morning with a vision. "I want to hang *Chandeliers* over the canals of Venice." From his early days at RISD, he had been placing his glass artworks in installations, groupings meant to change or transform a space. But working with a city as a site for sculpture would be a gigantic undertaking. What better place to try it out than Venice, where glass is an old tradition and a present-day art?

Dale Chihuly, *Palazzo di Loredana Balboni Chandelier,* **1996, 11 x 6 ft., Venice**

LEFT: Dale Chihuly, *Chandelier Drawing*, 1997, 60 x 40 in.

RIGHT: Dale Chihuly, *Ponti Duodo e Barbarigo Chandelier*, 1996, 11 x 4 ft., Venice

1996 *CHANDELIERS* OVER VENICE, ITALY

By *Chandeliers* Dale did not mean light fixtures hanging from a ceiling. Chihuly *Chandeliers* are large sculptures of specially blown glass. They look light and airy, almost as if they could float away. You'd never guess that some can weigh thousands of pounds.

Dale thinks big. He brought boxes to Venice containing parts for fourteen *Chandeliers*. With them came a team trained to put the *Chandeliers* together and install them. Dale said, "Hang glass in space and it becomes mysterious. It defies gravity and appears as something out of the ordinary."

The *Chandeliers* were an overwhelming success. In a courtyard, against a wall of golden stone, on the deck of a stately palace, or over a walking bridge, the *Chandeliers*' extravagant shapes and colors fit right in these old-world settings. But they

37

added a modern touch by changing familiar scenic views into something fresh. They also changed the momentum of Dale's career. These days, many museums, gardens, and collectors hang Chihuly *Chandeliers* from their ceilings.

2000 TOWER OF DAVID MUSEUM, JERUSALEM, ISRAEL, ALSO KNOWN AS THE CITADEL

The place was a restored seven-hundred-year-old medieval fortress, now the Tower of David Museum. There were ancient walls, ramparts, towers, minarets, catwalks, arches, and walkways. To get ready, Dale visited five times to make drawings. "Everywhere I looked at the site, there was something else I planned to do."

He did not arrive in Jerusalem alone. A team of thirty people included his partner, Leslie Jackson, and their young son, Jackson, whom Dale liked to call Mighty. With them came ten thousand pieces of carefully packed glass. They were met by a group of one hundred local workers—welders, architects, and engineers—who would assemble this huge installation.

On one of his ever-present big sheets of paper, Dale drew a piece that he called *White Tower*. He gestured to an archway. "It needs to go there," and that was enough explanation for his team. Afterward, one of the team pointed to the completed *White Tower*. "Comes from one sketch to something real. On paper it is only eight inches high, not tall, but that's the challenge. To make what Dale wants."

Dale Chihuly with *White Tower*, Jerusalem, 1999

LEFT: An aerial view of *Chihuly in the Light of Jerusalem 2000*, 1999, Jerusalem

RIGHT: Dale Chihuly and Jackson Chihuly, Jerusalem, 1999

Dale rejoiced in revising on the spot, perfecting his work. This is what he calls "the force, the magic, the joy of glass."

A few months after the grand opening, Dale returned to Jerusalem, this time with twenty-six monster cubes of ice from Fairbanks, Alaska. The cubes were so big they had to be moved by a fork-lift. Dale said, "There's a rhythm to ideas and I had wanted to use ice again for a long time." Delighted, he peered into the giant blocks. "They're all different, but they're all transparent. They're luminous."

The blocks were piled up to build an ice wall, thirteen to seventeen feet high and flooded with colored lights. "The ice wall is the biggest project I ever put up in my life. Celebratory."

Dale added, "I don't know what I want people to think when they see this. I want them to think what they want to think."

In the hot Jerusalem weather, the wall lasted for three glorious days and three nights before it melted away.

Over a million visitors came to see what Dale Chihuly had created.

GLASSHOUSES

Dale already was working on a project in Chicago when he visited the Garfield Park Conservatory. There he was struck by another inspiration. Why not place his glass pieces among the plants in this two-acre indoor garden? "I've always had an

Dale Chihuly, *Jerusalem Wall of Ice*, 1999, 13 x 54 ft., Jerusalem

interest in glasshouses. They are an ideal background for my work because I am able to bring it inside and at the same time surround it with nature." Park officials weren't hard to convince. They liked the idea. Soon *Towers* and *Floats* nestled among the rare plants. The resulting exhibit opened in November 2001 and ran for a year to record-breaking crowds.

From the beginning of his career, Dale had the idea of moving his artworks into less-traditional places. The public was dazzled not only by the small glass pieces poking through plants in the conservatory, but also by the large-scale sculptures and installations inside and out. "If you do a show in a museum you go from gallery to gallery. Here it's much more of a surprise," said Dale.

Garfield Park gave him yet another idea. Back in Washington, at the Tacoma Art Museum, Dale and his crew set up his first installation of *Mille Fiori*, adapted from *millefiori*—Italian for "one thousand flowers." This artwork had 879 colorful pieces of glass, which rose up like stems of plants or long-necked birds. They twirled and curled, enfolding and wrapping around each other, drawing the viewer into an explosion of glass forms.

Dale Chihuly, *Peacock Blue Tower,* **2001, 17 x 7 ft., Garfield Park Conservatory, Chicago**

Dale Chihuly, *Mille Fiori*, 2012, 10 x 58 x 20 ft. *Chihuly Garden and Glass*, Seattle

2017 NEW YORK BOTANICAL GARDEN

One by one the tractor trailers pulled out of an anonymous warehouse in Tacoma, Washington. They carried crates and cartons of Dale's glass, stored there to be ready for exhibitions. Six trucks headed 2,800 miles to a garden in New York City, where an exhibit was going on display.

The New York Botanical Garden, which includes 250 acres and a large, stately glasshouse, is open almost every day. Dale's team and helpers from the garden worked in full view of the public. Four expert workers installed a glass sun Dale named *Sol del Citrón*. A small cart arrived loaded with cartons. On each carton was a photograph of the glass shapes inside. The workers unpacked them and placed the new arrivals

43

ABOVE: Dale Chihuly, *Sol del Citrón*, 2014,
14 x 14 x 14 ft., the New York Botanical Garden,
Bronx, New York, installed 2017

RIGHT: Installing *Sol del Citrón*, the New
York Botanical Garden, Bronx, New York, 2017

OPPOSITE: Dale Chihuly, *Sapphire Star*, 2010,
9½ x 9½ x 9½ ft., the New York Botanical Garden,
Bronx, New York, installed 2017

on a mat. Golden-yellow curving pieces called horns
and shorter ribbed pieces (hornets) were picked up
one by one and wired onto the frame. *Sol del Citrón*
shone over the garden for six months before the parts
were packed back into boxes to return home.

Glass sculpture on a busy city street, in a
historic site, or placed among natural plants
in a glasshouse—what do these varied installations
have in common? All made of glass, Chihuly's artworks can be found in unexpected ways and places.

CHAPTER 8
THERE'S NO PLACE LIKE HOME

"I want people to be overwhelmed with light and color in a way they've never experienced before." —Dale Chihuly

Dale Chihuly's work is everywhere in Seattle and Tacoma, including a pedestrian bridge, Chihuly Bridge of Glass. At the Seattle Center is his masterpiece: a garden and glasshouse at the foot of the Space Needle.

Dale Chihuly, *Glasshouse*, 2012, and *Pacific Sun*, 2011, *Chihuly Garden and Glass*, Seattle, installed 2012, with partial view of the Space Needle

Dale Chihuly,
*Chihuly Garden and
Glass*, 2012, Seattle

Dale Chihuly, *Crystal Towers*,
Chihuly Bridge of Glass, 2002,
40 ft. tall, Tacoma, Washington

LEFT: Dale Chihuly, *Cattails*, *Niijima Floats*, and *Citron Icicle Tower*, 2012, *Chihuly Garden and Glass*, Seattle

RIGHT: Dale Chihuly, *Chiostro di Sant'Apollonia Chandelier*, 1995, *Mercato del Pesce Chandelier II*, 2012, and *Drawing Wall*, 2012, *Chihuly Garden and Glass*, Seattle, installed 2012

CHIHULY GARDEN AND GLASS, SEATTLE, 2012

Dale consulted with architects and landscape designers before settling on his own plan. A crumbling fun house arcade was torn down to make way for eight galleries. Outside are gardens filled with glass *Fiori* among the natural plants. Inside, his series over the years are on exhibit, including slumping *Baskets* and *Persian Ceiling*. Visitors also can go to the café to see some of Dale's Americana collections. These include ceramic dogs, bottle openers, old radios, dollhouse furniture, and toy soldiers. Dale's exuberance, sense of fun, and great eye for display can be seen wherever you look.

Beyond the café you can follow a long covered walkway strung with glittering *Chandeliers* that leads to a grand forty-foot-high glasshouse. With arching white metal beams and sweeping space, it has been compared to a cathedral. Hanging from the ceiling and gleaming in reds, oranges, and amber is the longest glass sculpture Chihuly has ever created.

Outside, along with the glass pieces sprouting amidst blooming flowers, are large-scale sculptures. A tall tower pulls the viewer into an aura of color

LEFT: Tin toys, the Boathouse, Seattle, 2012

RIGHT: Carnival chalkware figurines in Collections Café, *Chihuly Garden and Glass*, Seattle, 2012

and form. *Chihuly Garden and Glass* is one of the biggest tourist attractions in Seattle, a place that melds the natural and man-made world. It is a visual celebration of light and color. There were many glowing articles and reviews about Dale and his work.

In 2017, Dale and his wife, Leslie, who is president of Chihuly Studio, went public about the artist's battle with bipolar disorder that had begun in his early twenties and has continued off and on through the years. Leslie told reporters that they hoped Dale's success in spite of a chronic illness "might be helpful for other people."

"When I'm up I'm usually working on several projects," said Dale. "When I'm down I kind of go

**ABOVE: Leslie and Dale
Chihuly, the Boathouse
hotshop, Seattle, 2015**

LEFT: Dale Chihuly,
Glasshouse Sculpture
(detail), 2012, 27 x 100 x
23 ft., *Chihuly Garden and
Glass*, Seattle

into hibernation." He went on to say, "I'm lucky I like movies. If I don't feel good I'll put on a movie."

Dale's gift to himself in both good times and bad has been following his passions and fulfilling his creativity. Along the way he has worked with hundreds of talented people who have shared his vision. Dale's gift to the world is the joy of his creations. Nothing is dark. His art speaks about beauty and hope. When you pause before one of his gigantic glass sculptures, you are drawn in by the color, the glow, the way the light plays on the glass. The sheer size. It is a WOW experience!

Dale has said that in order to get better at glassblowing, an aspiring artist must do it over and over again. "You're making something that's never been made before. It's an ancient craft that someone invented two thousand years ago. Can you imagine blowing human breath down a blowpipe and getting a bubble and then heating it up in fire, using a couple of little tools and then making forms you can't touch? All you have to do is blow glass once and you want to become a glassblower."

Dale Chihuly with *Walla Wallas*, Venice, 1996

NOTES

PROLOGUE

"I think water": Dale Chihuly in *Chihuly Short Cuts* (video).

"Come on sweetheart": Dale Chihuly in *Chihuly Short Cuts* and *Chihuly Gardens & Glass* (videos).

"Makes this river": *Chihuly Gardens & Glass* (video).

"He was right there": Dale Chihuly in *Chihuly Baskets* and *Chihuly at the Royal Botanic Gardens, Kew* (videos).

CHAPTER 1

Puget Sound is a large inlet from the Pacific Ocean that stretches down the coast of Washington.

"Since I was a little boy": Burgard, Timothy Anglin, "Chihuly the Artist: Breathing Life into Glass," 1.

"I like to say": anecdote told to the authors in June 2017.

Marbles: anecdote told to the authors in June 2017.

Lawn-mowing business: anecdote told to the authors in June 2017.

CHAPTER 2

"I don't think much about the past": *Chihuly Gardens & Glass*, 32.

"She didn't make much": Susan Resneck Pierce, *Arches*, "Interview with Dale Chihuly '63."

"She was a great mother": Pierce, "Interview with Dale Chihuly '63."

"Sometimes we put out a street light": Pierce, "Interview with Dale Chihuly '63."

"My mother never told me": *Morning News Tribune* (Tacoma).

"I don't know how": *Morning News Tribune* (Tacoma).

"I played some sports": Mark McDonnell. Interview with Dale Chihuly. "Kitchen Sessions."

"I did sort of": McDonnell. Interview with Dale Chihuly. "Kitchen Sessions."

"I unfortunately joined": McDonnell. Interview with Dale Chihuly. "Kitchen Sessions."

"because I knew there would be" Pierce, "Interview with Dale Chihuly '63."

"just traveling, wandering." Pierce, "Interview with Dale Chihuly '63."

CHAPTER 3

"Sometimes I would be able": McDonnell. Interview with Dale Chihuly. "Kitchen Sessions."

"I was never very good": McDonnell. Interview with Dale Chihuly. "Kitchen Sessions."

"When I got there": Peter West, director, "Chihuly Projects" (rough cut, unreleased video).

"I was too intimidated": West, "Chihuly Projects" (rough cut, unreleased video).

—Note—The Acropolis is an ancient site on the highest point in the Greek city of Athens. The site's structures include the Parthenon and the ruins of the temple of the goddess Athena.

—Note—Israel was established in 1948 as a Jewish state following Germany's surrender in WWII and the tragic loss of six million Jewish people killed during the Holocaust. Located in the Negev desert, Kibbutz Lahav is near Israel's border with Jordan. Although Dale Chihuly is not Jewish, he was drawn to kibbutz life and acknowledges how significant his time there was working with so many brave, motivated young people.

"I remember": *Chihuly Jerusalem 2000*, 28.

"After the kibbutz experience": *Chihuly Jerusalem 2000*, 28.

"To this day": *Chihuly: On Fire*, 11.

Harvey Littleton, a well-known glass artist, started the glassblowing program at University of Wisconsin.

"to blow glass full time": *Chihuly: Color, Glass and Form*, 16.

James Carpenter: An American artist and a RISD student who collaborated with Dale on projects for four years. *20,000 Pounds of Ice and Neon* (1971) was their first large-scale installation. Carpenter also taught at the Pilchuck Glass School.

CHAPTER 4

"I learned from other artists that it wasn't that hard to make art. You do what you want to do. You just have to have the confidence to do it." *Chihuly at the Royal Botanic Gardens, Kew* (video).

—Note—The land for Pilchuck was owned by local art patrons Anne Gould Hauberg and John Hauberg. *Chihuly: On Fire*, 202.

—Note—In 1975, Dale and Seaver Leslie collaborated as two of the artists in residence that year at Artpark, located in upstate New York.

"There was no despair": Quotes on the accident from Chihuly Workshop Archives.

"It probably made me realize": Joselyn Art Museum, *Chihuly Inside and Out* (video).

"The thing I found most remarkable": Quote from Benjamin Moore, a pioneering glassblower who has worked with Chihuly, including on Chihuly's *Baskets* series in 1977 *Chihuly Baskets* (DVD).

CHAPTER 5

"I don't care what people call them—containers, sculpture, craft, fine art": "Chihuly the Artist: Breathing Life Into Glass."

"Most of the drawings are quite spontaneous": Chihuly, "Works on Paper," www.chihuly.com/work/works-paper.

"He is interested": Paula Stokes to authors 2017.

—Note—centrifugal force: An object traveling in a circle that behaves as if it is experiencing an outward force.

CHAPTER 6

"Imagine the sand turns into liquid": *Dale Chihuly: The Colors of Life*, YouTube.

—Note—Chihuly visited Santa Fe for the first time in 1974. He was invited by Lloyd Kiva New (1916–2002), who was then the art director of the Institute of Indian Arts and a distinguished designer and scholar, to set up a hotshop in an old barn on the campus. There, Dale introduced a group of young Native American students to glassblowing. Some years later a former student at the institute, Tony Jojola of the Isleta Pueblo in New Mexico, enrolled in Pilchuck Glass School and renewwed his association with Chihuly. With Dale's support, Tony also joined as an artist in residence at the Hilltop Artists program in Tacoma, Washington. Today, Tony Jojola is a successful glass artist, whose work is exhibited in galleries and museums. From *Chihuly Taos Peublo*, the exhibition catalogue/book by Lloyd Kiva New, 10–13.

In 1994 Dale helped his friend Kathy Kaperick (a local artist and gallery owner) start Hilltop Artists in the Tacoma public schools with twenty students. Students ages twelve to twenty receive full tuition to explore the glass arts, including mosaics, fusion, flameworking, and glassblowing. Hilltop Artists now has nine programs in various public schools and serves over 650 students each year. For more information about Hilltop Artists see www .hilltopartists.org.

This is a partial list of some of the many talented people with whom Dale has worked and developed close relationships.

Cylinders. Early work done by Kate Elliott, then Flora C. Mace. She was the first woman to teach at Pilchuck Glass School. Mace and Joey Kirkpatrick met at Pilchuck in 1979. Kirkpatrick and Mace have worked together for more than twenty-five years, producing a wide range of wood, stone, and glass sculptures.

James Mongrain worked on *Cylinders*, *Persians*, and *Ikebana*. In 1999, Dale choose him as lead gaffer because he liked to work larger and so does Dale.

Benjamin Moore is a pioneering glassblower who has worked with Chihuly over the years, including on Chihuly's *Baskets* series in 1977. He has served as director and teacher at the Pilchuck Glass School.

Italo Scanga (1932–2001) was an important friend and artistic mentor from Providence, Rhode Island.

William Morris arrived at the Pilchuck Glass School in 1978 and found work initially as a driver. Later, he worked with Chihuly and became his chief gaffer in the 1980s. Morris remained with Chihuly for ten years before deciding to form his own studio and develop his own artistic style of glassblowing.

William Morris and Richard Royal worked on overlapping series. Royal worked with Chihuly as a main gaffer for years and now works independently as a successful glassblowing artist. His work is exhibited in a number of museums.

Martin Blank is a successful glass artist who is exhibited internationally. He worked with Chihuly on the *Persians*.

Pino Signoretto (1944–2017) was considered one of the great glassblowers from Murano, Italy. He collaborated with Chihuly on the *Putti* series beginning in 1989.

Lino Tagliapietra is a Venetian glassblower who has also worked extensively in the United States. He collaborated with Chihuly on the *Venetians* series beginning in 1998 and enjoyed it so much that he returned many times to work with Chihuly.

"Dale began collecting Navajo blankets": Dale Chihuly, *Chihuly Cylinders* (DVD).

Dale collects Navajo and trade blankets. Starting in the seventeenth century, trade blankets were manufactured by various companies, especially for trade with Native American tribes.

"I pushed the idea of the transparency of glass": Dale Chihuly, *Seaforms*, 8.

The *Persians* were inspired by a group of paintings by Italian painter Vittore Carpaccio (1450–1526) called the *Persians* that Chihuly had seen in Venice. Dale Chihuly, *Chihuly's Persians* (DVD).

"Some of the color combinations": Dale Chihuly, *Chihuly Macchia*, 8.

"Normally I don't like . . . figures in glass": Dale Chihuly, *Chihuly Putti* (DVD).

"If the piece has separate parts": Dale Chihuly, *Chihuly Mille Fiori*, 4.

"In later Ikebana": Dale Chihuly, *Chihuly Macchia*, 8.

"We don't know if it will break. . . . more interesting": Dale Chihuly in *Chihuly Gardens & Glass* (video).

CHAPTER 7

"I've always had an interest": Dale Chihuly in *Chihuly Gardens & Glass* (video).

"I want to hang chandeliers": Dale Chihuly in *Chihuly Chandeliers & Towers* (DVD).

—Note—Glass was made in Venice dating back to the city's start in the early centuries following the fall of the Roman Empire (476 CE). There the glassmakers developed new processes that were secrets closely guarded from the rest of the world. During one period in the late middle ages, glassblowers were not permitted to leave the city.

"Hang glass in space": Dale Chihuly, *Chihuly Chandeliers & Towers*, 87.

"Everywhere I looked at the site": Dale Chihuly in *Chihuly in the Light of Jerusalem* (video).

"It needs to come from there": Dale Chihuly in *Chihuly in the Light of Jerusalem* (video).

—Note—Tower of David Museum, also known as the Jerusalem Citadel, is located in Jerusalem near the Jaffa Gate. This historic series of connected buildings and ruins dates back more than 2,000 years and reflects the tumultuous and complicated history of the city.

"Comes from a sketch": *Chihuly Short Cuts* (video).

"the force, the magic": Ibid

"There's a rhythm to ideas": Ibid

"They're all different": Ibid

"The ice wall is the biggest": Chihuly in *Chihuly in the Light of Jerusalem* (video).

"If you do a show": Dale Chihuly in *Chihuly Mille Fiori* (DVD).

CHAPTER 8

—Note—The Space Needle was built in 1961 for the 1962 World's Fair in Seattle. Including the antenna spire, it measures 605 feet high. The Space Needle has become the symbol of the city.

"I want people to be overwhelmed": *Chihuly Gardens & Glass*, 37.

—Note—"might be helpful for other people."

Although it was known to the teams, Dale and Leslie Chihuly spoke publicly for the first time about his struggles with a bipolar disorder to the Associated Press on March 22, 2017. In part it was because

they didn't want to leave out an important aspect of his legacy, but also as the result of a letter from a former employee, who claimed to have contributed without credit to the artist's work and then demanded money. The Chihuly Studio denied the claim. In June 2019 the judge dismissed the suit.

"You're making something that's never been made before": Dale Chihuly in *Chihuly Short Cuts* (video).

SELECTED BIBLIOGRAPHY

BOOKS AND EXHIBITION CATALOGUES

Adams, Henry. *Chihuly: On Fire*. Seattle: Chihuly Workshop, 2016.

Burgard, Timothy Anglin. *The Art of Dale Chihuly*. San Francisco: Chronicle Books and the Fine Arts Museums of San Francisco, 2008.

Chihuly, Dale. *Chihuly: An Artist Collects*. Seattle: Chihuly Workshop; New York: Abrams, 2017.

Chihuly, Dale. *Chihuly: Color, Glass and Form*. Tokyo, San Francisco, New York: Kodansha International Ltd., 1986.

Chihuly, Dale. *Chihuly Gardens & Glass*. Seattle: Portland Press, 2002.

Chihuly, Dale. *Chihuly Projects*. Seattle: Portland Press; New York: Abrams, 2000.

Chihuly, Dale. *Fire*. Seattle: Portland Press, 2006.

Ebony, David, Mark McDonnell, and Tim Richardson. *Chihuly Garden Installations*. Seattle: Chihuly Workshop; New York: Abrams, 2011.

Kuspit, Donald. *Chihuly: Volume I (1968–1996)*. Seattle: Portland Press, 1997.

Kuspit, Donald. *Chihuly: Volume II (1997–2014)*. Seattle: Chihuly Workshop; New York: Abrams, 2014.

New, Lloyd Kiva. *Chihuly Taos Pueblo*. Seattle, Washington: Portland Press, 1999.

INTERVIEWS

McDonnell, Mark. Interview with Dale Chihuly. "Kitchen Sessions," typescript of interview. March 15, 1998. Chihuly Studio Archives, Seattle.

Pierce, Susan Resneck, President Emeritus of University of Puget Sound. "Interview with Dale Chihuly, '63." *Arches* (University of Puget Sound alumni magazine), 2000.

ESSAYS IN MULTIMEDIA COMPILATIONS

Hoving, Thomas. "Reflections on Dale Chihuly." In *Chihuly Fire & Light*, 10–17. Seattle: Portland Press, 2010.

Taragin, Davira S. "Chihuly's *Fiori*: Magical Gardens." In *Chihuly Mille Fiori*, 4–15. Seattle: Portland Press, 2010.

Taragin, Davira S. "Chihuly's *Persians*: Remembrances of Venice." In *Chihuly's Persians*, 4–15. Seattle: Portland Press, 2010.

Taragin, Davira S. "*Cylinders* and *Soft Cylinders*: Chihuly's Canvases." In *Chihuly Cylinders*, 4–15. Seattle: Portland Press, 2010.

Taragin, Davira S. "Exploring Nature." In *Chihuly Seaforms*, 4–15. Seattle: Portland Press, 2010.

Taragin, Davira S. "Gravity's Pull." In *Chihuly Baskets*, 4–15. Seattle: Portland Press, 2009.

Taragin, Davira S. "A Passion for Flowers." In *Chihuly Ikebana*, 4–15. Seattle: Portland Press, 2010.

Taragin, Davira S. "Poetic Assemblages of Glass & Steel." In *Chihuly Chandeliers & Towers*, 4–15. Seattle: Portland Press, 2010.

Taragin, Davira S. "Three-Dimensional 'Canvases' of Exuberant Color." In *Chihuly Macchia*, 4–15. Seattle: Portland Press, 2010.

Taragin, Davira S. "A Touch of Mischief." In *Chihuly Putti*, 4–15. Seattle: Portland Press, 2009.

VIDEOS

Chihuly at the Royal Botanic Gardens, Kew. DVD. Directed by Peter West. Seattle: Portland Press, 2006.

Chihuly Gardens & Glass. DVD. Directed by Peter West. Seattle: Portland Press, 2004.

Chihuly in the Hotshop. DVD. Directed by Peter West. Seattle: Portland Press, 2007.

Chihuly in the Light of Jerusalem. DVD. Directed by Peter West. Seattle: Portland Press, 2004.

Chihuly Inside and Out. Joselyn Art Museum.

"Chihuly Projects," rough cut (unreleased). Directed by Peter West; produced by Portland Press.

Chihuly Outside. DVD. Directed by Peter West. Seattle: Chihuly Workshop, 2012.

Chihuly Over Venice. DVD. Directed by Gary Gibson. Seattle: KCTS Television, 1998.

Chihuly Short Cuts. DVD. Directed by Peter West. Seattle: Chihuly Workshop, 2017.

Dale Chihuly: The Colors of Life. YouTube.

Video Shorts on Chihuly and Workshop by Peter West, vimeo.com/user25444452.

NEWSPAPER

Chihuly, Viola, quoted by Joan Brown. "Molten Magic: Dale Chihuly's Mystical Artist Sensitivity Flows and Glows in Scintillating Glass." *The [Tacoma] Morning News Tribune*, 8 Sept. 1991, 12.

Johnson, Gene. "Interview with Dale and Leslie Chihuly." Associated Press. March 22, 2017. apnews.com /5acce34113af46deb3d4db6be2c5c6a9

WRITINGS ABOUT DALE CHIHULY

Burgard, Timothy Anglin. "Chihuly the Artist: Breathing Life into Glass." 2008. www .Chihuly.com/life/writings /chihuly-artist-breathing-life-glass

AUTHORS' CONVERSATIONS AT CHIHULY STUDIO AND WORKSHOP AND PILCHUCK GLASS SCHOOL, SEATTLE, JUNE 5–7, 2017:

Dale Chihuly

Leslie Jackson Chihuly: President and CEO of Chihuly Studio and Workshop

Diane Caillier: Vice President, Chihuly Studio and Workshop

Ken Clark: Archivist, Chihuly Studio

Goretti Kaomora: Senior Graphic Designer and Brand Manager

Paula Stokes: Manager, Hotshop and Special Projects

WHERE TO SEE ARTWORKS BY DALE CHIHULY

SELECT MUSEUMS AND GALLERIES WITHIN THE UNITED STATES

Birmingham Museum of Art, Birmingham, Alabama

Jule Collins Smith Museum of Fine Art, Auburn University, Auburn, Alabama

Mobile Museum of Art, Mobile, Alabama

Arizona State University Art Museum, Tempe, Arizona

Phoenix Art Museum, Phoenix, Arizona

Scottsdale Center for the Performing Arts, Scottsdale, Arizona

Arkansas Arts Center, Little Rock, Arkansas

Crystal Bridges Museum of American Art, Bentonville, Arkansas

Art, Design & Architecture Museum, University of California, Santa Barbara, California

Berkeley Art Museum, University of California, Berkeley, California

Crocker Art Museum, Sacramento, California

de Young Museum, San Francisco, California

Los Angeles County Museum of Art, Los Angeles, California

Mingei International Museum, San Diego, California

Museum of Contemporary Art San Diego, La Jolla, California

Orange County Museum of Art, Santa Ana, California

Palm Springs Art Museum, Palm Springs, California

San José Museum of Art, San Jose, California

Colorado Springs Fine Arts Center, Colorado Springs, Colorado

Denver Art Museum, Denver, Colorado

Museum of Outdoor Arts, Englewood, Colorado

Lyman Allyn Art Museum, New London, Connecticut

New Britain Museum of American Art, New Britain, Connecticut

Wadsworth Atheneum Museum of Art, Hartford, Connecticut

Yale University Art Gallery, New Haven, Connecticut

Delaware Art Museum, Wilmington, Delaware

Boca Raton Museum of Art, Boca Raton, Florida

Center for the Arts, Vero Beach, Florida

Imagine Museum, St. Petersburg, Florida

Leepa-Rattner Museum of Art, St. Petersburg College, Tarpon Springs, Florida

Lowe Art Museum, University of Miami, Coral Gables, Florida

Museum of Arts and Sciences, Daytona Beach, Florida
Museum of Fine Arts, St. Petersburg, Florida
Naples Museum of Art, Naples, Florida
Norton Museum of Art, West Palm Beach, Florida
NSU Art Museum, Fort Lauderdale, Florida
Polk Museum of Art, Lakeland, Florida
Ringling College of Art and Design, Sarasota, Florida
Samuel P. Harn Museum of Art, University of Florida, Gainesville, Florida
Wiener Museum of Decorative Arts, Dania Beach, Florida
Albany Museum of Art, Albany, Georgia
Columbus Museum, Columbus, Georgia
High Museum of Art, Atlanta, Georgia
Hilo Art Museum, Hilo, Hawaii
Honolulu Museum of Art, Honolulu, Hawaii
Krannert Art Museum, University of Illinois, Champaign, Illinois
Museum of Contemporary Art, Chicago, Illinois
Rockford Art Museum, Rockford, Illinois
Brauer Museum of Art, Valparaiso David Owsley University, Valparaiso, Indiana
Children's Museum of Indianapolis, Indianapolis, Indiana
David Owsley Museum of Art, Ball State University, Muncie, Indiana
Fort Wayne Museum of Art, Fort Wayne, Indiana
Indianapolis Museum of Art, Indianapolis, Indiana
Charles H. MacNider Art Museum, Mason City, Iowa
Marianna Kistler Beach Museum of Art, Kansas State University, Manhattan, Kansas
Spencer Museum of Art, University of Kansas, Lawrence, Kansas
Wichita Art Museum, Wichita, Kansas
Speed Art Museum, Louisville, Kentucky

New Orleans Museum of Art, New Orleans, Louisiana
Portland Museum of Art, Portland, Maine
Addison Gallery of American Art, Andover, Massachusetts
deCordova Sculpture Park and Museum, Lincoln, Massachusetts
Museum of Fine Arts, Boston, Boston, Massachusetts
Smith College Museum of Art, Northampton, Massachusetts
Springfield Museum of Fine Arts, Springfield, Massachusetts
Detroit Institute of Arts, Detroit, Michigan
Flint Institute of Arts, Flint, Michigan
Frederik Meijer Gardens & Sculpture Park, Grand Rapids, Michigan
Besser Museum for Northeast Michigan, Alpena, Michigan
Kalamazoo Institute of Arts, Kalamazoo, Michigan
Krasl Art Center, St. Joseph, Michigan
Muskegon Museum of Art, Muskegon, Michigan
Minneapolis Institute of Arts, Minneapolis, Minnesota
Daum Museum of Contemporary Art, Sedalia, Missouri
Kemper Museum of Contemporary Art, Kansas City, Missouri
Museum of Art and Archaeology, University of Missouri, Columbia, Missouri
Saint Louis Art Museum, St. Louis, Missouri
Saint Louis University Museum of Art, St. Louis, Missouri
Springfield Art Museum, Springfield, Missouri
Lauren Rogers Museum of Art, Laurel, Mississippi
Missoula Art Museum, Missoula, Montana
Joslyn Art Museum, Omaha, Nebraska
Currier Gallery of Art, Manchester, New Hampshire
Morris Museum, Morristown, New Jersey

Museum of American Glass at WheatonArts and Cultural Center, Millville, New Jersey
Newark Museum, Newark, New Jersey
Princeton University Art Museum, Princeton, New Jersey
Albright-Knox Art Gallery, Buffalo, New York
Brooklyn Museum, Brooklyn, New York
Cooper Hewitt, Smithsonian Design Museum, New York, New York
Corning Museum of Glass, Corning, New York
Everson Museum of Art, Syracuse, New York
LongHouse Reserve, East Hampton, New York
Memorial Art Gallery, University of Rochester, Rochester, New York
Metropolitan Museum of Art, New York, New York
Museum of Arts & Design, New York, New York
Whitney Museum of American Art, New York, New York
Asheville Art Museum, Asheville, North Carolina
Mint Museum, Charlotte, North Carolina
Plains Art Museum, Fargo, North Dakota
Akron Art Museum, Akron, Ohio
Cincinnati Art Museum, Cincinnati, Ohio
Cleveland Museum of Art, Cleveland, Ohio
Columbus Museum of Art, Columbus, Ohio
Contemporary Arts Center, Cincinnati, Ohio
Dayton Art Institute, Dayton, Ohio
Milan Museum, Milan, Ohio
Toledo Museum of Art, Toledo, Ohio
Edmond Fine Arts Institute, Edmond, Oklahoma
Oklahoma City Museum of Art, Oklahoma City, Oklahoma
Portland Art Museum, Portland, Oregon
Carnegie Museum of Art, Pittsburgh, Pennsylvania

National Liberty Museum, Philadelphia, Pennsylvania
Palmer Museum of Art, Pennsylvania State University, University Park, Pennsylvania Philadelphia Museum of Art, Philadelphia, Pennsylvania
Reading Public Museum, Reading, Pennsylvania
David Winton Bell Gallery, Brown University, Providence, Rhode Island
Rhode Island School of Design Museum, Providence, Rhode Island
Columbia Museum of Art, Columbia, South Carolina
Art Museum of South Texas, Corpus Christi, Texas
Art Museum of Southeast Texas, Beaumont, Texas
Austin Museum of Art, Austin, Texas
Dallas Museum of Art, Dallas, Texas
Jesuit Dallas Museum, Dallas, Texas
Museum of Fine Arts, Houston, Houston, Texas
San Antonio Museum of Art, San Antonio, Texas
Hunter Museum of American Art, Chattanooga, Tennessee
Utah Museum of Fine Arts, University of Utah, Salt Lake City, Utah
Chrysler Museum of Art, Norfolk, Virginia
Virginia Museum of Contemporary Art, Virginia Beach, Virginia
Virginia Museum of Fine Arts, Richmond, Virginia
Allied Arts Association, Richland, Washington
Experience Music Project, Seattle, Washington
Henry Art Gallery, Seattle, Washington
Jundt Art Museum, Gonzaga University, Spokane, Washington
Museum of Art, Washington State University, Pullman, Washington
Museum of Glass, Tacoma, Washington
Museum of Northwest Art, La Conner, Washington

Wenatchee Valley Museum & Cultural Center, Wenatchee, Washington
Northwest Museum of Arts and Culture, Spokane, Washington
Seattle Art Museum, Seattle, Washington
Tacoma Art Museum, Tacoma, Washington
Washington State Historical Society, Tacoma, Washington
Whatcom Museum of History and Art, Bellingham, Washington
Renwick Gallery, Smithsonian Institution, Washington, D.C.
White House Collection of American Crafts, Washington, D.C.
Arts Centre, Martinsburg, West Virginia
Huntington Museum of Art, Huntington, West Virginia
Leigh Yawkey Woodson Art Museum, Wausau, Wisconsin
Haggerty Museum of Art, Marquette University, Milwaukee, Wisconsin
Milwaukee Art Museum, Milwaukee, Wisconsin
Racine Art Museum, Racine, Wisconsin

SELECT MUSEUMS AND GALLERIES OUTSIDE THE UNITED STATES

AUSTRALIA
Art Gallery of Western Australia, Perth, Australia
National Gallery of Australia, Canberra, Australia
National Gallery of Victoria, Melbourne, Australia
Powerhouse Museum, Sydney, Australia
Queensland Art Gallery, South Brisbane, Australia

CANADA
Art Gallery of Greater Victoria, Victoria, British Columbia, Canada
Canadian Craft Museum, Vancouver, British Columbia, Canada

Canadian Clay & Glass Gallery, Waterloo, Ontario, Canada
Royal Ontario Museum, Toronto, Ontario, Canada
Montreal Museum of Fine Arts, Montreal, Quebec, Canada

ENGLAND
Victoria and Albert Museum, London, England
World of Glass, St. Helens, England

IRELAND
Ulster Museum, Belfast, Northern Ireland

NEW ZEALAND
Auckland Museum, Auckland, New Zealand
Dowse Art Museum, Lower Hutt, New Zealand
Hawke's Bay Exhibition Centre, Hastings, New Zealand
Te Manawa, Palmerston North, New Zealand
Waikato Museum, Hamilton, New Zealand

ACKNOWLEDGMENTS

Many people helped along the way to make this book a reality. It began as an idea, really an inspiration, while viewing Dale Chihuly's installation at the Missouri Botanical Garden in 2003. Although there have been many books and videos about Chihuly's beautiful glass sculptures and smaller glass objects, there was no book for young readers about his work. Our heartfelt gratitude goes to the artist and his wife, Leslie Jackson Chihuly, for inviting us into their world of glass. We are grateful to Chihuly's amazing team, who organized our three days in Seattle and made sure we didn't miss a thing, including a wonderful lunch/interview with Dale and Leslie. We were given a glassblowing demonstration in the hotshop followed by tours of the Boathouse, Workshop, and Studio, where we observed the process that Chihuly has masterminded over the years to create his innovative body of work. Members of the team graciously read and checked our texts and images. We could not have accomplished the book without them. A special thank you to good friend Pam Ebsworth, who introduced our books to the Chihulys.

The other team that has been indispensable is the group at Abrams Books: the indomitable Howard Reeves, our longtime editor at Abrams; editorial assistant Emily Daluga, who patiently showed us how to navigate the complicated (to us) editing software; editorial assistant Sara Sproull, who spent hours organizing the flow of images we chose from the Workshop and many other tasks too long to mention; designer Steph Stilwell, who was determined with us to make the book colorful and fun for kids; freelance designer Katie Benezra; managing editor Marie Oishi; production manager Erin Vandeveer; and art director Pamela Notarantonio.

PHOTOGRAPHY

David Aschkenas, Theresa Batty, Dick Busher, Shaun Chappell, Dale Chihuly, Jan Cook, Kaley Ellis, David Emery, Claire Garoutte, Donna Goetsch, Russell Johnson, Robin E. Kimmerling, Scott Mitchell Leen, Roger Ligrano, Teresa Nouri Rishel, Terry Rishel, Roger Schreiber, Robert Vinnedge, Mark Wexler, Ray Charles White, Charlie Wilkins, Nathaniel Willson

INDEX